Phobias

Titles in the Diseases and Disorders series include:

Acne
AIDS
Allergies
Alzheimer's Disease
Anorexia and Bulimia
Anthrax
Anxiety Disorders
Arthritis
Asthma
Attention Deficit Disorder
Autism
Bipolar Disorder
Birth Defects
Blindness
Breast Cancer
Cerebral Palsy
Childhood Obesity
Chronic Fatigue Syndrome
Cystic Fibrosis
Deafness
Dementia
Diabetes
Down Syndrome
Dyslexia
Epilepsy
Fetal Alcohol Syndrome
Food Poisoning
Growth Disorders
Headaches
Heart Disease
Hemophilia

Hepatitis
Hodgkin's Disease
Human Papillomavirus (HPV)
Leukemia
Lou Gehrig's Disease
Lyme Disease
Mad Cow Disease
Malaria
Malnutrition
Measles and Rubella
Meningitis
Mental Retardation
Mood Disorders
Multiple Sclerosis
Muscular Dystrophy
Obesity
Ovarian Cancer
Parkinson's Disease
Prostate Cancer
SARS
Schizophrenia
Sexually Transmitted
    Diseases
Sleep Disorders
Smallpox
Strokes
Teen Depression
Toxic Shock Syndrome
Tuberculosis
West Nile Virus

DISEASES & DISORDERS

Phobias

Jenny MacKay

LUCENT BOOKS
A part of Gale, Cengage Learning

GALE
CENGAGE Learning™

Detroit • New York • San Francisco • New Haven, Conn • Waterville, Maine • London

GALE
CENGAGE Learning™

LIBRARY OF CONGRESS CATALOGING-IN-PUBLICATION DATA

MacKay, Jenny, 1978-
  Phobias / by Jenny MacKay.
    p. cm. — (Diseases and disorders)
  Includes bibliographical references and index.
  ISBN 978-1-4205-0103-2 (hardcover)
  1. Phobias—Juvenile literature. I. Title.
  RC535.M33 2009
  616.85'225—dc22
<div align="right">2008033762</div>

Lucent Books
27500 Drake Rd.
Farmington Hills, MI 48331

ISBN-13: 978-1-4205-0103-2
ISBN-10: 1-4205-0103-8

Printed in the United States of America
1 2 3 4 5 6 7 12 11 10 09 08

Table of Contents

"The Most Difficult Puzzles Ever Devised"

Charles Best, one of the pioneers in the search for a cure for diabetes, once explained what intrigued him so about medical research: "It's not just the gratification of knowing one is helping people," he confided, "although that probably is a more heroic and selfless motivation. Those feelings may enter in, but truly, what I find best is the feeling of going toe to toe with nature, of trying to solve the most difficult puzzles ever devised. The answers are there somewhere, those keys that will solve the puzzle and make the patient well. But how will those keys be found?"

Since the dawn of civilization, nothing has so puzzled people—and often frightened them, as well—as the onset of illness in a body or mind that seemed healthy before. Being unable to reverse conditions such as a seizure, the inability of a heart to pump, or the sudden deterioration of muscle tone in a small child, or even to understand why they occur was unspeakably frustrating to healers. Even before there were names for such conditions, before they were understood at all, each was

7

a reminder of how complex the human body was and how vulnerable.

While our grappling with understanding diseases has been frustrating at times, it has also provided some of humankind's most heroic accomplishments. Alexander Fleming's accidental discovery in 1928 of a mold that could be turned into penicillin has resulted in the saving of untold millions of lives. The isolation of the enzyme insulin has reversed what was once a death sentence for anyone with diabetes. There also have been great strides in combating conditions for which there is not yet a cure. Medicines can help AIDS patients live longer, diagnostic tools such as mammography and ultrasounds can help doctors find tumors while they are treatable, and laser surgery techniques have made the most intricate, minute operations routine.

This "toe-to-toe" competition with diseases and disorders is even more remarkable when viewed in a historical continuum. An astonishing amount of progress has been made in a very short time. Just two hundred years ago, the existence of germs as a cause of some diseases was unknown. In fact, less than 150 years ago a British surgeon named Joseph Lister had difficulty persuading his fellow doctors that washing their hands before delivering a baby might increase the chances of a healthy delivery (especially if they had just attended to a diseased patient)!

Each book in Lucent's Diseases and Disorders series explores a disease or disorder and the knowledge that has been accumulated (or discarded) by doctors through the years. Each book also examines the tools used for pinpointing a diagnosis, as well as the various means that are used to treat or cure a disease. Finally, new ideas are presented—techniques or medicines that may be on the horizon.

Frustration and disappointment are still part of medicine because not every disease or condition can be cured or prevented. But the limitations of knowledge are constantly being pushed outward; the "most difficult puzzles ever devised" are finding challengers every day.

Senseless Fears

Human beings have a love/hate relationship with fear. Medals are given to valiant warriors who charge fearlessly into combat, while those who sneak around whimpering in their battle helmets are labeled cowards and in some cultures are even put to death for what is considered a war-time crime. As a whole, people generally find fear to be disgraceful.

At the same time, people are fascinated by fear. In fact, they pay money to be scared out of their wits. They wait in long lines to see horror movies in theaters and to scream their lungs out on amusement park rides. Reality television shows such as *Fear Factor* recruit people to do unthinkably scary things. Fear has become an industry.

A lesser-known fact is that fear is a widespread health problem. Millions of people do not seem to have an "off" switch when it comes to being afraid. They do not need to watch a scary movie or bungee jump off of a bridge to panic—they do it at the sight or even the thought of a certain thing or situation that petrifies them. They cannot put their fear out of their mind. They have what doctors and scientists call a phobia.

Phobias are as ancient as fear itself. The Greeks believed that senseless fears were the mischievous work of Phobos, the god of fright. (*Phobos* is the root of the modern word *phobia*.) The Greeks also believed that the god of nature, Pan, loved to spread fear, and this is where the modern word *panic* comes from.

The Greek physician Hippocrates recorded stories of people with unusual phobias over 2,400 years ago.

Stories of phobic people date back at least 2,400 years, when the ancient Greek physician Hippocrates wrote about a peculiar man named Damocles who would not go near the edge of a ditch for any reason. Hippocrates also wrote about another man, an enemy of the Greek conqueror Alexander the Great, who was struck by horror if he heard anyone playing the flute after dark.

The ancients believed these seemingly senseless fears were the work of the gods. They had no other explanation for what could make an otherwise sensible, respectable man tremble at the sight of something that was not dangerous. These days, the ancient problem continues. There are common fears of everything from horses to hailstorms and dinner parties to public toilets. In more than two thousand years, doctors have not made a great deal more progress at explaining this problem than Hippocrates did.

Doctors of the human mind have examined many possible causes of phobias. In the early 1900s, psychologist Sigmund Freud believed that these senseless fears, like almost everything else that goes on in the mind, are tied to hidden sexual feelings. Some of his peers, meanwhile, did not bother to understand their fearful patients but merely dulled their panic attacks with opium.

No one—Hippocrates, Freud, or anyone in between—has yet come up with an answer that fits. One of the few things doctors do know about phobias is that they are fearfully common. Even today, they are everywhere. There is also evidence that our ancestors are, at least in part, to blame for the strange disorder, since phobias seem to run in families. Sons and daughters with phobic parents often grow up to suffer from phobias themselves. It has been said that they learn these fears, but there have also been studies of twins separated at birth who have the same phobia. A single, certain cause of phobias has yet to be found.

Phobias can strike anyone at any time. No one is immune. Certain types of phobias are more common at certain ages or in certain stages of life, but all phobias are unpredictable phenomena. Phobic reactions are far worse than the kind of fear people experience riding a roller coaster or watching a scary movie. They involve panic so extreme that the person has no control over it. People with phobias describe fainting, throwing up, sweating, clenching their hands, being unable to breathe, and feeling like they are having a heart attack or dying. The

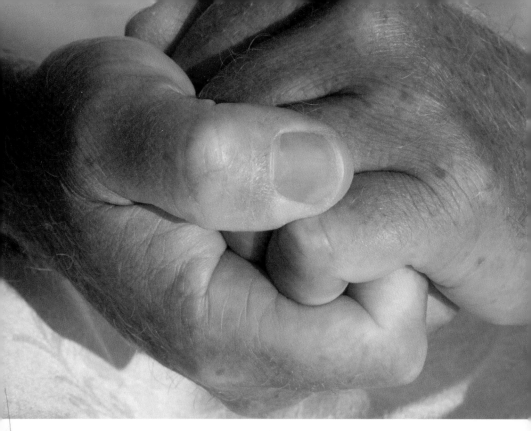

Clenched hands are among the many physical reactions people with phobias can have when experiencing feelings of panic.

experience is as scary and senseless to them as the thing that set off the phobia. Phobics usually realize that their fear is not reasonable, but this gives them no control over it.

Actually curing the condition seems as unpredictable as phobias themselves. It can be so difficult to root out the source of the fear that many people just find ways to live with it, often developing very strange behaviors to avoid the thing that triggers their panic. These behaviors can have ill effects. They can keep phobics from traveling, for example, or from going to college, dating or marrying, or having their dream job. In this way, fear can truly ruin lives.

Some desperate people seek help for phobias in extreme forms, plunging headfirst into their fear to force themselves to get over it. Modern technology gives people more options for this kind of treatment than Hippocrates had to offer. Computer-simulated experiences are among the new ways people try to get over senseless but powerful fears. Using virtual technology, a modern-day Damocles can simulate standing on the edge of the Grand Canyon and look his fear in the eye. Technology could be what finally changes the fate of phobias.

Still, there is not yet a standard cure for a condition that has existed for thousands of years. Fear is widely studied but poorly understood. The ancient phenomenon of phobias is still alive and well.

CHAPTER ONE

What Is a Phobia?

Everyone is afraid of something. From the moment of birth, humans can experience fear. Almost all newborn babies are terrified by loud noises and seem to dread falling, even if they have never been dropped. They get over these fears as they grow, but they pick up new ones on their journey through childhood. Studies have shown that 40 percent of kids can name something that terrifies them. By the time they become adults, 17 percent of people still cling to at least one fear.

Fright is both natural and useful. The world is full of things that cause harm. Being scared of these things makes people avoid them so they might live to see another day. Even animals use fear to survive. A rabbit that panics at the sight of a coyote, for instance, will probably live longer than a rabbit that dashes across open fields without caution.

People, of course, do not live with the same kinds of dangers that plague rabbits and other creatures. Unless they swim in shark-infested water or get lost in Africa where there are man-eating predators, there is little need to worry about things with pointed teeth. Yet, most people have a healthy respect for any creature with claws or fangs, even people who live in cities and encounter very few wild animals outside of a zoo. Having *some* fear of certain things is normal and natural.

Human fears, however, do not always serve a survival purpose. It is one thing to be scared of something that is actually dangerous, such as falling off a cliff or getting buried in an avalanche. But many people fear things they know could not possibly harm or kill them. Some people lie awake at night fretting endlessly about an upcoming meeting or test. Others chew their fingernails at the thought of giving a speech to an audience. Some become anxious and start to sweat in small rooms, even if a window is open and they know there is plenty of air. When fears like these, which have nothing to do with survival, start to take over a person's life, they become a real problem. These fears are phobias.

Life-Changing Fears

Most people can name at least one thing that really unnerves them, but not every fear is a phobia. A true phobia is a fear that transforms a person's life. People who have phobias are so frightened of the thing that scares them, they will do almost anything to avoid it. Phobias force people to make choices they might not make if it were not for their fear.

Take Stephanie and Logan, two teenagers who dislike spiders. If Stephanie sees a spider, she screams, waves her arms, and runs around the room until it crawls into a crack or someone comes along and kills it. Only then can she sit down and relax. No doubt, Stephanie has a strong fear of spiders, but she does not have a phobia.

Compare Stephanie's behavior to Logan's. He does not have to see a spider to experience fear. Even the mere thought of a spider bothers him so much that he has not worn shorts or sandals in nine years. He wears pants, heavy socks, and shoes all the time just to make sure no spider could possibly touch his bare skin. He rips all the covers off of his bed every evening to search for spiders, then makes the bed again before going to sleep with the light on. He sets his alarm clock to go off every hour so he can check the ceiling for spiders throughout the night.

Logan has never gone camping, because there might be spiders in the tent. Logan neatly folds and stacks his dirty laundry in the hamper instead of throwing it on the floor, where spiders might crawl into his socks or T-shirts. Logan has few friends.

He refuses to spend the night at anyone else's house—after all, other houses might not have been sprayed for spiders. Logan has a phobia.

According to Edmund J. Bourne, author of *The Anxiety and Phobia Workbook*, many people develop a fear of some situation or thing during their lifetime, but "only when you start to *avoid* that situation or object," he says, "do you *learn* to be phobic."[1] By definition, phobics are habitual avoiders. Some avoid specific things or situations that scare them. Others avoid people. And some phobics are afraid of fear itself.

Specific Phobias

The most common type of phobia is triggered by only one thing, usually an object, animal, or situation. These phobias are called specific phobias, or sometimes simple phobias, because the cause of the fear is simple to identify. People with this kind of phobia know exactly what scares them.

A specific phobia, also known as a simple phobia, is the fear of one specific thing. Fear of spiders, for example, is a specific phobia.

"A person can develop a specific phobia of anything," says Lynne L. Hall, writing in *FDA Consumer*. "In most cases, the phobia is shared by many and has a name. Animal phobias are common. And, of course, there's the fear of flying (pterygophobia), heights (acrophobia), and confined spaces (claustrophobia)."[2] The fears Hall describes fit into two of the main categories of specific phobias—fears set off by some sort of animal and fears sparked by a certain kind of situation.

Logan's fear belongs in the first category: specific phobias of animals. It is classified as a simple phobia because the source of the fear is very specific and easy to define—for Logan, it is anything with eight legs growing out of a thorax. But Logan almost surely would not agree that his fear is simple. Most of his daily choices, beginning with what he is going to wear in the morning and ending with how he is going to get through the night, are made with spiders in mind.

Many people have arachnophobia, a fear of spiders. In spite of their small size and skittish nature, spiders are some of the most hated creatures on Earth. They share their bad reputation with many other cold-blooded critters. Snakes, for example, strike terror into the hearts of ophidiophobes. For scoleciphobes, the terror-causing villain is worms. Ichthyophobes, people who fear fish, might well live their whole lives without ever taking a dip in a lake or the ocean in order to avoid the thing that frightens them.

Animal phobias can be triggered by warm-blooded creatures, too, even those commonly considered to be pets. Leporiphobes, for instance, are afraid of bunnies (some, of the Easter Bunny in particular). An alektorophobe is afraid of chickens. Playwright William Shakespeare and Roman emperor Julius Caesar are among the people throughout history who have lived in terror of cats, and a cynophobe gets skittish around dogs. Nearly every type of animal, in fact, has a specific phobia named after it. But as common as animal phobias are, they are not the only source of the hundreds of specific phobias that have been identified.

Famous Fearfuls

About one-third of the world's population suffers from life-changing fears. Even the rich and famous are not immune.

Film director Martin Scorsese refuses to travel in a plane unless he can first work out safe weather patterns for the flight path. If he cannot satisfy himself that there will be a good landing, he will not go. (He once missed accepting a best-director award for this reason.)

Johnny Depp, the actor who portrayed Edward Scissorhands, Captain Jack Sparrow, and Sweeney Todd, is afraid of clowns.

In the movie *Kill Bill: Vol. 2*, the screams of actress Uma Thurman, who was being buried alive, were no act at all—she's claustrophobic.

Soccer star David Beckham dreads things that are out of order—so much so that he buys clothing to match his furniture.

Author Anne Rice of *Vampire Chronicles* fame is scared of the dark, and singer-actress Barbra Streisand's stage career took a three-decade intermission while she struggled with a bad case of stage fright.

Phobias are an everyday problem, and not just for everyday people.

Actor Johnny Depp is one of many famous people who has revealed a personal phobia. For Depp, it is a fear of clowns.

Fear of Situations

Some people who fear animals might be afraid to stray too far from a city sidewalk, because they are paralyzed by the thought of an encounter with the creature they fear. People with a different kind of simple phobia may also avoid nature, but it might be a situation, not an animal, that petrifies them—a situation such as getting trapped in a storm or ending up high on the side of a mountain.

Novelist Patrick McGrath, author of the book *Spider*, is not afraid of spiders at all, but of something else entirely—high

Many people attempt to manage their phobias by avoiding a specific situation. For example, a person with a fear of heights is likely to avoid going on a mountain hike.

places. He says his fear of heights has kept him from doing certain things, such as hiking up mountains, for most of his life.

"As a small child I fell out of a tree, broke my wrist, and was knocked unconscious," he says. He believes that experience caused his fear, which has "become stronger and stronger, to the point where I can't watch rooftop scenes in movies."[3]

McGrath says he once suffered an attack of vertigo, the dizzy feeling that scares people with acrophobia (a fear of heights), during a drive through the mountains with his wife and stepson. "I realized to my horror that the road had turned into a narrow gravel track and was climbing steeply with no barrier rail up the sheer cliff-face," he says. "After about ten yards I was dripping with sweat, my knuckles were white, and I had to face the fact that I was terrified and couldn't go forward. . . . I just had to reverse down onto safe ground."[4]

Fear of being in a situation can be even more troublesome than fearing an animal. People who are terrified of sheep, for example, can quite easily avoid them in day-to-day living, as long as their home is not a sheep farm. People with a fear of high places or crowded spaces, on the other hand, might have a harder time, especially if they live in a city. When elevators, stairwells, or crowded subway trains set off the kind of sweaty panic attacks McGrath says he suffers when he gets too high in the air, life in a city may be hard indeed.

Still, specific phobias of animals and situations are, for most people, manageable. Those who have these phobias know exactly what frightens them, and they quickly learn how to avoid panic-spurring objects or circumstances. A specific phobia of an animal or situation can make a person choose carefully where to go and what to do, but the fear is usually something he or she can control and cope with. This is not always the case for people with the third kind of simple phobia: a fear of natural phenomena.

Fear of Natural Phenomena

Thunderstorms, tornadoes, earthquakes, and other natural events can happen almost anywhere, sometimes with little or

Weather phobias, such as a fear of tornadoes, can be particularly debilitating because these events are unpredictable, rendering some people afraid to leave their homes if a storm is forecasted.

no warning. People with specific phobias of natural phenomena, therefore, usually feel they have very little control over their fear. They cannot prevent a thunderstorm or predict when an earthquake might happen, and therefore, there is no guarantee that they can avoid it. They may cope by staying indoors most or all of the time, a behavior that affects their quality of life.

"There are people who are so debilitated by the thought of severe weather that they can't drive their cars or go to work or school," says psychologist John Westefeld, who has studied people who fear thunderstorms and tornadoes. "That extreme reaction has all the characteristics of a phobia."[5]

It is possible for some people with phobias of natural phenomena to limit how often they are exposed to what frightens them. Someone with a phobia of tornadoes, for instance, probably would not choose to live in Oklahoma, a state where these storms are common. Other types of natural phenomena, such as wind, are much more widespread and difficult to avoid, and people with phobias of such things may often feel trapped by their fear.

Westefeld says he has met people who are so afraid of the weather, they own special weather radios to check constantly for looming storms. Some have told him they start to worry when a storm is still a week away. People with weather phobias might even call in sick to work or school on the day of a storm because they are too afraid to go outside. Such a phobia can make life difficult when the person has to start inventing excuses for missing too much work or school.

Fear of Illness

People who fear natural phenomena may use sickness as their excuse for staying indoors, but some people fear a sick day itself. Terror at the thought of getting hurt or becoming ill is the fourth type of simple phobia, and it is one of the most common and troublesome.

Fiona Rittigan has such a phobia, and she explains what it is like to live with a fear of getting sick. "I've got a very very bad phobia about germs," she says. "I find it very difficult to touch anything. . . . And I can't bear people coughing in front of me as I'm very scared of illness."[6] For people like Rittigan, phobias of germs can create many problems. Handling money, opening doors, answering telephones, and shaking people's hands are terrible experiences for them. They are so worried about getting sick that it becomes difficult to interact with other people and to do normal, everyday activities.

Other people with illness-related phobias do not dread germs themselves, like Rittigan does, but instead have a fear of going to the doctor. For many phobics, it is the thought of a needle, a lab coat, or a stethoscope that sends them over the edge. These people may fear medical professionals and procedures so much that they refuse to make appointments even for routine check-ups such as caring for their teeth.

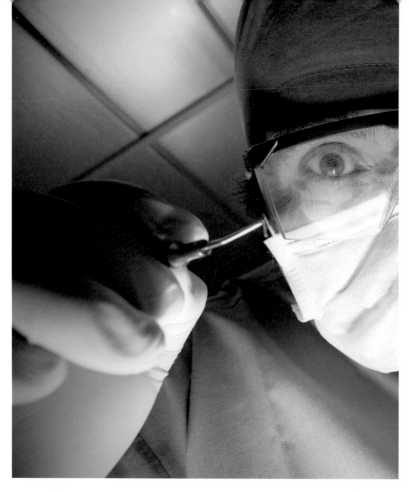

Fear of dentists is a common phobia that leaves those who suffer from it willing to risk the health of their teeth in order to avoid having to go through an exam or procedure.

In fact, says psychologist Sheryl Jackson, "one of the most common phobias is the fear of dentists." She says people who suffer with this phobia "will literally let their teeth rot out because they are afraid to go to a dentist."[7] This phobia of dentists or other doctors may date back to childhood and a painful experience with a wisdom tooth or a medical test. Sometimes, however, phobic patients fear doctors and dentists for another reason entirely. Some phobics are afraid of saying or doing something painfully *embarrassing* in front of their doctor. This fear of embarrassment is not a simple phobia at all. It belongs to an entirely different family of phobias, called social phobias. A social phobia is a fear of what other people think.

Social Phobias

When nine-year-old Nicole moved with her mother to a new city, she started to dread school. Her worries about her new class kept her up at night. She stopped eating and drank six cans of soda every day. She began faking illnesses so she could stay home from school. It was obvious that something was very, very wrong.

"Nicole has been tearfully refusing to go to school because she 'wants to go home' and is 'scared to go back' to her classroom,"[8] says psychology professor Thomas G. Plante in his

A fear of using a public restroom is among many types of social phobias that restrict some people's ability to do certain things outside of their home or in the company of others.

Name That Fear

Hundreds of specific phobias have been named. Some are much more common than others. Here are a few of the most bizarre:

arachibutyrophobia: fear of peanut butter sticking to the roof of the mouth

blennophobia: fear of slime

cacophobia: fear of ugly things

cegophobia: fear of work

euphobia: fear of getting good news

genuphobia: fear of knees

hippopotomonstrosesquippedaliophobia: fear of long words

leukophobia: fear of the color white

macrophobia: fear of long waits

octophobia: fear of the figure 8

panophobia: fear of everything

rhytiphobia: fear of getting wrinkles

testophobia: fear of taking tests

syngenesophobia: fear of relatives

xylophobia: fear of wood

New phobias are being named all the time. Added to the list in recent years are things like perdetophobia (fear of not saving your work before your computer crashes), frigensophobia (fear that your cell phone is hurting your brain), and lattephobia (fear of complex coffee shop menus).

book, *Contemporary Clinical Psychology*. These are classic early signs of a social phobia.

More than 5 million people in the United States live with some kind of social phobia, and for most of them, their fears started out much like Nicole's. Many phobics, at an early age, begin to feel terribly uneasy around other people, especially if they have to do something in front of someone—give a speech, introduce themselves, or even walk past a large group. A social phobia makes a person worry nonstop that others are watching him, judging him, or laughing at him. And because the world is full of people, a social phobia is very hard to ignore. There is no avoiding it. Everywhere one goes and everything one does, someone might be watching.

"Typically, your concern is that you will say or do something that will cause others to judge you as being anxious, weak, 'crazy,' or stupid,"[9] says Bourne. We all feel nervous sometimes, but Bourne says that for social phobics, this concern is much stronger than the situation calls for.

People develop all sorts of social phobias. Some fear eating in front of other people because they might choke or spill on themselves. Some are afraid of taking tests. The fear of writing in front of someone, even just signing a paper, is a common social phobia. Other people are so uncomfortable with the idea of using a public restroom that they find it hard to be away from home for a long period of time. One social phobia, though, appears more frequently than all the others: the fear of speaking in front of a group.

"The fear of public speaking is the most common social phobia," says Bourne. "In fact, this is the most common of all phobias."[10]

The fear of talking in front of people can be so strong that it affects major life choices such as the kinds of classes or colleges students choose or the kinds of jobs adults pick for themselves. Many people who have a fear of public speaking say they have turned down great opportunities, such as a special award or a promotion at work, because they would have had to give a speech to accept it.

Social phobias, such as the fear of public speaking or of public restrooms, are not equally strong for everyone. Some people who dread using public toilets, for example, can force themselves to do it when there is no other choice, but for others, a public bathroom is never an option. Some people with a fear of public speaking can manage to do it in front of very small groups, but for some, the fear is so strong that they struggle to talk to even one other person. All social phobias, though, make it hard to live normally. According to Bourne, "you would be given a formal diagnosis of social phobia only if your avoidance interferes with work, social activities, or important relationships."[11] A fear is only labeled a phobia when it begins to direct a person's day-to-day decisions or affect the way he lives his life.

Social phobias are usually much harder to live with than specific phobias, because it is more difficult to avoid people than it is to stay away from a particular object or situation. Still, even social phobias usually cause stress only in certain circumstances. If a woman is terrified by public restrooms, then attending a baseball game at a large stadium may be totally out of the question, but she might still be able to visit public places as long as they have private bathrooms.

Some phobics have such an extreme case of fear that they find it hard to go anywhere public at all. They worry that if they leave home, they will panic, and their fear of fear itself erases their chances of having a normal life. These people have the worst and most complicated fear of all—agoraphobia.

The Fear of Being Afraid

When a thirty-three-year-old woman named Nora had a panic attack in the middle of a grocery store, she felt like she was being strangled. Her heart raced. She felt dizzy. She had no choice but to leave her cart in the middle of the aisle and run for the door and the fresh air outside. It was the first in a series of panic attacks that left Nora wondering whether she would ever feel safe outside of her home again.

People with agoraphobia may avoid leaving their homes for fear of encountering something that prompts a panic attack, and for fear of being embarrassed if a panic attack strikes with other people around.

"She felt that if she wasn't careful, she could bring on another attack," says Raeann Dumont in her book, *The Sky Is Falling: Understanding and Coping with Phobias, Panic, and Obsessive-Compulsive Disorders*. "An underlying belief of an agoraphobic is 'I am vulnerable, the world is a dangerous place, and I need someone to take care of me.'"[12]

Agoraphobia, the fear of open spaces, is considered the worst of all phobias. It is marked by nearly nonstop terror that a panic attack will strike. If it does, the person with agoraphobia fears she will not be able to escape the situation that sets off the panic, or if she does manage to escape, she fears that it will be embarrassing. The panic attack might happen on a subway train, for example, where escape is impossible, or it could happen in the middle of a wedding, where escape would be humiliating. Either way, the attack would be horrifying to the person. Agoraphobics are so afraid of panicking unexpectedly that they often feel anxious leaving home at all, even for a short while. Lisa Capps and Elinor Ochs, authors of *Constructing Panic: The Discourse of Agoraphobia*, say that "agoraphobic persons often describe feeling trapped by an ever-present threat of panic and their belief that they cannot risk leaving safe havens such as home."[13]

Agoraphobia is a crippling condition. People who suffer from it feel afraid almost all the time. Some are even afraid of being in their own homes by themselves and want a relative or a close friend with them always. The fact that their fear is not logical does not make it go away. They understand that they are not really in any danger, yet they panic just the same. When they become too fearful to even leave home, their lives become very lonely and depressing.

Medical experts are trying to answer the question of what goes wrong in someone's mind to create this kind of fear. Scientists who study human behavior want to know who gets phobias, what causes them, and how they can be treated.

CHAPTER TWO

Who Gets Phobias?

Phobias trouble people all over the world. In her book, *Phobias: Fighting the Fear*, Helen Saul says phobias "are truly international, crossing the boundaries of language and culture."[14] A New Yorker who fears airports and everything that soars out of them has a different phobia than an African tribesman who screams at the sight of any snake that slithers into his family's hut, but the feelings of panic they both experience are very similar.

Anyone can develop a phobia—men and women, teens and young adults, an elderly lady or a one-year-old boy. People who suffer from these uncontrollable fears are often laughed at and ridiculed, especially if the thing they fear—dust, for example, or flowers or balloons—is something that is not typically dangerous. But phobias are no laughing matter, and having one does not make someone crazy. In fact, people who have phobias are usually very aware that their fears are not logical. A phobia is a mental disorder—a tendency to panic at the mere thought of a certain thing or situation. Phobias are believed to be one of the most common problems affecting the human mind.

Who's Afraid of the Big Bad Wolf?

People have long been interested in stories about weird terrors. Even fairy tales are full of phobias. In *The Emperor's New Clothes*, a dread of being unfashionable developed into a fear of public nudity, and the Pied Piper's promise to rid Hamelin of its rat problem probably came as a welcome offer to a town afflicted with musophobia, the fear of rodents.

An overwhelming fear of heights may cause some people to turn down a job that would require them to work in a skyscraper office building.

Fairy-tale author Hans Christian Andersen was himself neurotically phobic. Among the things that terrified him were dogs, scratches, and being buried alive. (He was known to leave notes on his bedside table at night to remind people he was not dead, just asleep.) So unusual were Andersen's problems that he was among the early phobia cases studied by psychologist Sigmund Freud in the late nineteenth century.

Absurd as Andersen's fears may seem, phobias like these are surprisingly common. According to the National Institute of Mental Health, 19 million Americans admit to having a specific phobia—a fear of one particular thing or situation, such as wasps or heights. This comes out to about 9 percent of the population, and these statistics do not include people who have a phobia but have not admitted it. Saul says the percentage might be even higher if more people were honest about their fears. Women have "consistently higher fear ratings than men," she says, but this is "possibly because men are less willing to admit to fears."[15]

Although a phobia can start at any age, specific ones usually take root in childhood. Fears of weather, natural disasters, or animals are most likely to start when a person is young. The fears most people have when they are kids wither over time, but for some, they grow into phobias. The most common age a specific phobia develops is seven years old. Some people's childhood fear never goes away, and by the time they are teenagers or young adults, they have a phobia.

"More often than not a phobia can start with a small concern, which grows into a worry and then builds to become a full-blown phobia," says journalist Madeleine Brindley. This fear, she says, "can have a negative effect on a person's life as it takes over and stops them from doing something that might, in fact, be enjoyable."[16]

Teenagers and adults can develop phobias, too, even of things that never bothered them as kids. These fears are especially puzzling because they seem to come out of nowhere. A sixteen-year-old who thought nothing of heights as a young kid might suddenly start to perspire heavily with fear on a roller coaster or a Ferris wheel. The unexpected terror, with no link to any frightening experience from his childhood, might be humiliating for him.

This teenager certainly would not be alone in his fear. More men than women have a phobia of heights, and it usually begins in the teenage years. The fear might not be a problem if a man simply learns to avoid Ferris wheels and roller coasters. If, however, a job requires him to work on the top floor of a high-rise building, he might be forced to make a major career choice because of his phobia, and this is what sets phobias apart from the normal jitters that bother the rest of us.

"Every person has had a fear or fears at some time in their life and will do so in the future," says Brindley. "It is how we deal with those fears that makes the difference."[17] For people with a true phobia, the urge to deal with the fear by avoiding the frightening object or situation overpowers other important things in their lives.

Phobias and Age

Humans fear different things at different ages. Many infants have irrational fears of strangers, or sometimes, of anyone who is not their mother. At eighteen months of age, a toddler is most likely to fear being away from his parents.

Kids who are four to six years old tend to be scared of imaginary stuff: monsters, ghosts, and the "thing under the bed."

By age seven, fear of the dark might shift to a fear of something more specific that can actually happen, such as a fear of getting caught in a storm, being bitten by a dog, or crashing on a bicycle.

At about age twelve, common fears shift again. Just in time for the teenage years, social phobias tend to take root. Fear of giving presentations in class, taking tests in front of a teacher, or going to school at all tend to crop up at about this time.

For some adults, childhood fears have not vanished. The older the fear, the harder it is to get rid of. Phobics learn ways to avoid situations or people that make them nervous, and these bad habits can be hard to kick.

A little girl checks for monsters under her bed, a fear of imaginary things that is typical among young children.

Fear of People

Although there are hundreds of specific phobias and only a handful of social ones, people who admit to fearing other people are nearly as common as those who have a specific phobia. Fifteen million Americans over the age of eighteen have some kind of social phobia—a fear of doing something in front of someone else.

"Recent studies suggest that social phobia affects 4 to 5 percent of the U.S. population," says author Edmund J. Bourne. "Up to 14 percent of adults experience social phobia at some time in their lives."[18] Because it is much more difficult to avoid other people than to steer clear of cliffs or closets, these social phobias take a bigger toll on the people who suffer from them.

Social phobias usually strike during the teenage years, between the ages of eleven and nineteen. Rarely do they appear later than a person's early twenties. Social phobias do, however, tend to get worse over time. Someone who developed a social phobia in her twenties will have more trouble with her phobia in her forties and fifties.

People with social phobias are sensitive to the scrutiny of others, and their fear of embarrassment can lead them to avoid situations where they are around other people.

One woman, whose fear of eating in public started when she was fourteen, has found it very hard to have a normal social life now that she is an adult. "When men ask me out I always say, 'I don't do dinner,'" she says. "I'm too embarrassed to admit the real reason—that I have panic attacks in restaurants."[19]

What makes this woman's fear a phobia is that it keeps her from living an otherwise normal life. She cannot go on dates. Business lunches are out of the question. She says she even makes up excuses when people invite her to eat out with them, telling them she cannot afford it. Her fear is more than a worry about spilling spaghetti in her lap or getting food stuck in her teeth. It is paralyzing. It affects the very way she lives her life.

"An attack feels like the world is closing in around me," she says. "I can feel the blood draining from my face. I go cold and start hyperventilating. I feel if I don't reach . . . safety in time, I'm going to die. It's absolutely terrifying."[20]

Men are even more likely than women to develop social phobias. They may fear all kinds of situations, from boardroom meetings at work to getting a haircut. In their book, *Anxiety Disorders and Phobias: A Common Perspective*, Aaron T. Beck and Gary Emery describe a man with a complicated social phobia: "His basic fear was present in other situations," they say, such as in church or in school auditoriums—but in particular, he feared barbers. "This man would run out of the barbershop just before his turn in the chair."[21]

Just as a specific phobia is much worse than merely feeling skittish about something, a social phobia is more than just being shy. In fact, not everyone with a social phobia *is* shy, except in certain situations such as restaurants or public restrooms. But in these situations, social phobics face powerful sensations of stress and panic. Many live in constant fear of embarrassment, whether they are men or women, adults or teens.

"People suffering from social phobia fear the scrutiny of others," says author Lynne L. Hall. "They tend to be highly sensitive to criticism, and often interpret the actions of others in social gatherings as an attempt to humiliate them. They are afraid to enter into conversations for fear of saying something foolish, and may agonize for hours or days later over things they did say."[22]

Some people with a social phobia eventually find it hard to leave the comfort and safety of home. It may become the only place they do not feel they are being watched and judged. In this way, people with severe social phobias are similar to agoraphobes.

Fear of Everything

The broad fear of panicking in any new situation keeps almost 2 million American adults stuck in their homes much or all of the time. The rarest of all phobias, affecting less than 1 percent of American adults, agoraphobia is also the worst. People with specific phobias and social phobias know what frightens them, but for people with agoraphobia, anything could set off a panic attack with little or no warning. Instead of worrying about the next thunderstorm or eating out or getting trapped in an elevator, agoraphobics worry about everything. Many of them spend their lives trying to avoid everything, too.

Psychiatrist John R. Marshall, says that for agoraphobes, everyday situations "take on a quality of danger, of being 'unsafe.'" Not surprisingly, he says, "many agoraphobics are homebound, unable to work, and often completely dependent on others." He describes one patient who traced her agoraphobia to three panic attacks she suffered in college. "By the time I met her," he says, "she had not crossed the threshold of her house for twenty years."[23]

Agoraphobia strikes most of its victims when they are in their twenties. About twice as many women as men suffer from the widespread terror it causes. Most people with agoraphobia suffer from a combination of specific phobias and social phobias, constantly feeling like they are in danger of a deadly disaster and also of getting laughed at by other people.

Agoraphobics have no control over the feelings of panic that can take over at any time. Many begin to believe they are going crazy or even dying. Their panic attacks make them feel like they are strangling, suffocating, or having a heart attack.

Agoraphobic people suffer from a variety of fears that are so debilitating that they may refuse to leave home for years at a time.

Agoraphobia usually gets worse over time, so that eventually, some who suffer from it never leave home.

"Agoraphobia is the most disabling of all the phobias," says Hall. "There are so many associated fears—the fear of crowds, of elevators, of traffic."[24]

People with complicated fears like these often feel they have no control over their condition. Unfortunately, they are usually right. Even doctors do not yet know exactly why some people suffer with disabling fears. Only some types of phobias can be traced to a specific experience or trigger.

Fear, in Numbers

1 in 10: estimated number of people who have a phobia

4%: percentage of people in the United States who suffer from a social phobia

3 million: number of people in the United States who have agoraphobia

2 to 1: ratio of women to men who have a specific phobia

7 years old: average age when specific phobias start

13 years old: average age when social phobias start

20%: percentage of specific phobias that go away on their own, without treatment

Common Triggers

The causes of any kind of phobia are not always clear. Certain experiences, however, do seem to spark certain fears. In particular, many people who have specific phobias can name the incident that set off their apprehension.

Julia Riddick, for example, can trace her strange phobia of buttons back to one childhood experience. "I've had this problem ever since I was a little girl," she says. "It began after I opened a drawer at home one day and saw a green cardigan with big buttons that gave me the creeps."[25] Another woman, Karen, links her fear of restaurants to an illness she had as a teenager. "It started when I was 14 and recovering from glandular fever," she says. "I hadn't been able to eat properly for several months so as soon as I could eat proper meals I went for it.

But my stomach had shrunk so I couldn't swallow all the food I was trying to cram in. After one particularly heavy meal, I had to run off to be sick. I was really ashamed and embarrassed, and I became so frightened of it happening again that I started avoiding eating in public."[26]

Getting attacked by a dog, coming down with an illness, or being trapped in a violent storm can set off a lifelong specific phobia. Social phobias, on the other hand, often have their roots in personality. Children who are shy often grow into teenagers who are self-conscious, says Saul. "Social phobia typically starts in the late teens, just when young people are establishing their identities and facing all sorts of social pitfalls,"[27] she explains. These teens, in turn, may become adults who fear social situations.

The widespread fear and anxious feelings of agoraphobia often start with the same kinds of worries that plague social phobics, such as embarrassment and fear of being teased. For agoraphobes, these fears are made worse by a traumatic event such as losing a loved one. Agoraphobics sometimes also have a specific phobia, as well, which may have started earlier in life than their agoraphobia. This has led doctors to think that the tendency to be afraid is part of some people's biology. In fact, whether their fear is specific or general, phobics of all kinds may have their parents to blame. Scientists who study phobias believe the senseless fears can be inherited. "Identical twins can develop the same phobia even if they are separated at birth and grow up in different places," says Elkins. "This suggests genes may be involved."[28]

The way people respond to fear might run in families for other reasons, too. A child who grows up watching her mother scream at the sight of any eight-legged creature will naturally think spiders are something terrifying. It seems that just growing up around someone with a phobia can trigger a phobia. Phobias may have more to do with how we see others responding to fear, than with our natural human tendency to be afraid of certain things. "Our fears may have nothing to do with our

A frightening experience as a child can sometimes lead to a person developing a phobia that lasts into adulthood.

biology," Saul says. "It is possible that we have learned them solely through careful observation of those around us."[29]

Some people's phobias are set off by something they have read about in a newspaper or seen on television. Many individuals are afraid of flying in an airplane, for example, even though they have never been in a plane crash. For some of these individuals, it is possible that just watching footage of an airplane crash on a television news program could trigger a phobia.

Not everyone suffers from a phobia, however, even though most people have seen frightening things in person or on TV. It is not clear why some people who have survived a car accident can continue to travel in cars without fear, while other people are terrified of having a car accident even when they have never experienced one. To better understand why some people have phobias and others do not, doctors and scientists are trying to understand the symptoms and the experience of terror that sets phobias apart from regular, day-to-day, sensible fears.

CHAPTER THREE

Living with a Phobia

When actresses in horror movies need to act panicked during a scary scene, they know exactly what to do. They open their eyes wide, gasp for air, and shriek, scream, and run. This continues until the actress either comes face to face with whatever is after her or the director shouts, "Cut!" Such panic may seem fake and overdone on screen, with the heroine stuck in a mode of fright that takes away her ability to think logically and often results in her untimely end. Viewers may wonder why the poor lady cannot snap out of it long enough to figure out how to unlock a door and escape.

A phobic, however, might think the actress does a fine job of showing the type of fear reaction that people with phobias suffer. This sweaty, heart-racing, gut-clenching blur of activity has deep roots in biology. *Panic* is another word for the fight-or-flight response that is automatic in all mammals, not just humans. When faced with a life-or-death situation, the body takes over and logic disappears. A chemical called adrenaline shoots through one's veins, eyes open wide, breathing speeds up, and the body prepares to either fight or run for life.

All phobics panic from time to time, even when this response is not actually helpful. Certainly, if someone is facing a wolf that is foaming at the mouth, it is reasonable to panic. Having the same reaction to a friendly circus clown handing out purple balloons does not make as much sense. For a person with a phobia of clowns or balloons, however, the second situation could easily set off the fight-or-flight response, complete with gasping, shrieking, and sprinting for the nearest exit like an actress in a horror film. Later, embarrassment is what horrifies the phobic, and he might start to avoid any place where he could encounter a clown or a balloon, because he fears embarrassing himself like that again. This is what it feels like to live with a phobia.

Signs of Dread

Phobic Peter Slip knows exactly when his fear began. "As a nine-year-old I can remember collecting earwigs in matchboxes, like kids do," he says. "They didn't worry me at all."[30] Then one day, as a teenager, he says he picked up a broken flagstone and came face to face with a squirming nest of earwigs. "I dropped

The physical results of a panic attack can include shortness of breath, chest heaviness and pain, a racing heartbeat, nausea, and a choking feeling.

the stone, my face went bright red and I started gasping for breath. I ran as fast as I could in the other direction although my legs felt like jelly and I thought I was going to collapse. I threw myself down on the grass to recover but immediately sprang up again, terrified that there were more earwigs nearby. Ever since, my whole life has been affected by a fear of earwigs."[31]

Some people with specific phobias remember the bad experience that started their fear—getting bitten by a dog, for example, or falling out of a tree, or being locked in a trunk by a cruel older sibling. Some specific phobias are set off when a parent, teacher, uncle, or other adult warns about the dangers of something, such as swimming in the deep part of a lake. Still other phobias come from watching TV, reading the newspaper, or hearing about something scary that happened to somebody else. And some of them seem to appear out of nowhere. In fact, says journalist Susan Stevens, "most people with phobias don't remember a traumatic encounter that triggered their fear."[32]

Whatever their cause, phobias are much more than just feeling nervous in a dangerous situation. A phobia sets off a complete panic attack, as if the person's very life were in danger. When this happens in a safe place, such as on a school bus, in a movie theater, or in the middle of a restaurant, the fear is completely out of proportion to the danger, and the memory of the panic is what ends up feeding the phobia. "Once you panic," says Stevens, "your physical reaction is etched into memory so you'll be ready for a similar threat in the future." This memory of fear is a problem for people with phobias, she says, because it "primes them to respond excessively to harmless situations."[33]

One thing most phobics agree on is that panicking is no picnic. The racing heartbeat, the tight chest, and the struggle to breathe are terrifying in themselves. Some phobics faint or throw up. Others think they are having a heart attack or are choking to death. When the panic attack is over, they start to fear that it will all happen again, so they go to great lengths to avoid whatever they believe sets off their panic attacks.

"I can't even sit down in my living room until I've taken out an insecticide spray and covered the whole room," says Slip.

Diagnosis: Phobia

Is it a phobia or just a fear?

The difference between the two is that phobias cause panic. If you have one or more of the following symptoms when you meet up with the thing you fear, you might have a phobia:

blushing

sweating

trembling

throwing up (or feeling as if you might)

shaky voice

clenched muscles

racing heart

difficulty breathing

diarrhea

cold hands

fainting

If you also go (far) out of your way to avoid what scares you and if you feel like your fear is keeping you from doing things you want to do, you may indeed be a phobic. You would not be alone. Millions of people admit to having absurd or unreasonable fears. (Perhaps millions more are too embarrassed to confess that they do.)

"I keep a spray in every room and hold a stock of extra cans just in case. It's no fun having to plan your life to avoid a tiny insect."[34]

Phobias are considered a psychological problem, one that begins somewhere deep in the mind. Some scientists think that people with phobias were born to have them, because these people are naturally more anxious and scare more easily than people who do not have phobias. This might be why phobias often seem to run in families—they are caused by something in a person's biology. Wherever a phobia comes from, however, once it has taken root in the mind, it is probably going to stay a while. "It can be hard to shake a phobia,"[35] says Stevens.

Young children who have specific phobias truly think their very life is in danger when they see the thing that scares them. As they grow up, they may start to realize that the object, animal, or situation is not deadly. For some people, this is the end of the phobia. For others, however, the realization that the object is not dangerous does not make the phobia go away. It only adds to the person's embarrassment about being afraid of it. This very embarrassment makes it hard for many people with specific phobias to get help for their problem. It might be just too humiliating to go to a doctor and say, "I am deathly afraid of shoelaces." The person may instead choose to suffer quietly and wear slip-on shoes for the rest of her life.

Doctors think that many specific phobias go unreported for exactly this reason—phobics do not want to admit to fears that they know are not sensible. Instead, they go through life quietly praying they do not have an embarrassing run-in with the object of their fear.

Sometimes, the fear of embarrassment itself becomes the true phobia, and this opens the door to a whole new class of fear, one that is much harder to live with. The thing that causes panic is other people, and the desire to avoid them can be a very serious problem.

The Faces of Fear

"When I think back on high school now, I can see myself getting more and more self-conscious, more and more buried in my work," says Julie, a patient with a social phobia. "It used to be I'd try to dig into my work and make the outside world disappear. But at some point it changed, and it was me I was trying to make disappear."[36]

A public gathering of friends may seem fun to most people, but for social phobics, it can cause overwhelming feelings of anxiety and dread.

This is how it might feel to be a social phobic—a person afraid of other people. In particular, social phobia amounts to a fear of what other people think. Everywhere a social phobic goes, she is worried about who might be watching her, judging her, or whispering about her. She frets nonstop about the way others see her, and when she leaves a party or other social situation, she may sit at home for long hours, worrying about the way she looked or acted or spoke.

"Anxiety," says author Helen Saul, "can make sufferers blush, sweat, shake, and draw attention to themselves by looking obviously uncomfortable—the very situation they wished to avoid at all costs."[37] These are the very same panic responses that strike people with specific phobias, except that they are not set off by something like a thunderstorm or the sight of a needle. The terror is triggered by people. "Simply stated," says psychiatrist John R. Marshall, social phobics "fear that they will make fools of themselves in public."[38]

Not everyone who has a social phobia wishes the rest of the world would just disappear. There are different kinds of social phobias. Some people feel very comfortable in crowds, as long as they do not have to eat anything. Some people are afraid of meeting strangers but are comfortable around people they already know. Some do not like to walk if they think people are watching them. Others are uncomfortable when they are shop-

Fear of public speaking, such as having to give a classroom presentation, is the most common social phobia.

ping. Even driving a car worries some social phobics—they are deeply troubled by the thought of angering other drivers or making anyone wait.

By far the most common social phobia is public speaking. There are more people with stage fright, than with any other kind of phobia, even spiders or heights or small spaces. Something about standing in front of a crowd and giving a speech makes most people nervous. For a social phobic, though, the intense fear of public speaking can cause many obstacles in life. Choices about careers, hobbies, and many other things are made with the fear in mind.

Julie, a brilliant physics student suffering from a social phobia, describes a hard choice she faced. She had only one thing left to do in order to graduate from college and become a physicist: She had to give a presentation about her final project. Even though she had spent years creating the project, and even though unveiling it to her instructors and fellow students was the ticket to getting a degree and her dream job, she claims that because of her phobia, it was impossible to make the presentation.

"It's crazy," she says. "I know I'm letting my whole career, my whole life, go down the drain. I've practiced my presentation hundreds of times. I could make it in my sleep to an empty room. But—I'm too afraid to do it."[39]

Why the thought of being in the spotlight makes so many people anxious is something that interests scientists. Human beings are naturally social creatures, so it does not make sense that at least five out of every one hundred people are so worried about embarrassing themselves that they cannot do some day-to-day things such as eating in a group. Some scientists think the problem may be linked to ancient history. The earliest humans, in order to survive harsh living conditions, simply *had* to be accepted by those around them. If they did not fit in with the group, they would be kicked out, and in those days, being all alone usually meant a person would be more susceptible to starvation, animal attacks, or exposure to the elements.

"Social phobics often feel—irrationally, they admit—that the social circumstances they fear have life-or-death meaning," says Marshall. "Fears of criticism or disapproval, of being deemed of low social worth and thus rejected, become fears of banishment."[40]

Wherever a social phobia comes from, people living with one are usually desperate for answers to the problem. Many, like Julie, have lived with a social phobia for as long as they can remember. They may feel that it is completely ruining their life. Their fears trap them in a lonely world of missed opportunities and unfulfilled dreams. Even more troubling, social phobias can get worse over time. What starts out as a fear of one kind of situation may grow into a fear of many situations.

Marshall describes one patient whose fear of eating in public began with an embarrassing situation at a dinner party when she was twelve. "During the course of the meal, she accidentally spilled food on the floor," Marshall says. "Enraged, her father forced her to place her plate on the floor and finish the meal there, saying, 'If you're going to act like a dog, then eat like a dog.'"[41] Marshall says the woman never again felt comfortable eating in front of other people. "Whenever she tried, she choked violently and sometimes even vomited. The fear of such episodes grew so intense that she became a near recluse."[42]

When a social phobia gets this strong, there are few situations that do not make the person squirm with dread. She may begin to feel uncomfortable leaving home at all. This may be how the widespread fear of agoraphobia starts. Like most people who have a phobia, agoraphobes suffer terrifying panic attacks. But the thing that sets off their panic is not one specific type of animal or place or experience. Instead, a panic attack is completely unpredictable. It can strike anywhere, at any time. The trigger could be anything at all. The person therefore may begin to fear not just one thing, but everything that is outside of his or her home.

Fear Everywhere

Agoraphobia is the fear of panicking. Feelings of panic are terrible, and most people who experience them are reacting to something truly dangerous. The danger is what they fear (and

Because a person with agoraphobia may not be able to predict when a panic attack might strike, she may decide that the only safe place to be is at home.

Triskadekaphobia: The Fear of Thirteen

The number thirteen has always had a rotten reputation. The trouble may date back to an ancient Norse myth of a dinner party gone bad when the twelve invited gods were joined by a nasty thirteenth guest who killed the god of joy.

For Christians, there is a similar tale. Judas, the betrayer of Jesus, was the thirteenth guest at the Last Supper.

According to ancient Romans, witches always gathered in groups of twelve. The thirteenth guest was none other than the devil.

Twelve has always been the more popular number. We have twelve months in a year and twelve signs in the Zodiac. There were twelve Greek gods of Olympus. But thirteen just seems to rub people the wrong way.

Modern skyscrapers rarely have a floor numbered thirteen. Many airports lack a gate with the number thirteen. In Florence, Italy, any street address that falls between twelve and fourteen is labeled "twelve and a half."

Do people really buy the hype about poor number thirteen? Economists say yes. U.S. companies lose a total of about $800 million every Friday the thirteenth because so many people refuse to travel, trade stock, or do other business on this day.

A panel of elevator buttons from a high-rise building shows the lack of a thirteenth floor.

in fact, the whole experience of panicking in the first place might later lead to a specific phobia).

Agoraphobics, on the other hand, sometimes panic for no good reason at all. They could be anywhere, doing even the most normal things, and start to panic. "I'm afraid to go out and *do* things," says Meg, a woman who lives with agoraphobia. "I told myself that I'm sure to *die* or *panic* or *whatever* if I get on an airplane or a freeway."[43]

Authors Lisa Capps and Elinor Ochs say agoraphobia "is a problem in how one relates to and understands objects in the world, including oneself."[44] Fearing everything, like Meg does, may be a sign that something has gone wrong with a person's natural fear and panic response. "Meg frequently laments her struggles to deal with situations that are 'not at all threatening to normal people' and her fear of doing things that are 'not at all frightening,'"[45] say Capps and Ochs.

Scientists believe that people with agoraphobia are naturally anxious to begin with. Add the fear of random and unpredictable panic attacks, and many who struggle with agoraphobia begin to find it difficult to leave their own home. They dread the idea of being trapped somewhere when panic sets in. For an agoraphobic person, any situation could bring on the kind of terror shown by an actress in a horror movie. It is embarrassing, it is frightening, and it is a true disability that can keep a person trapped in the few places where he or she feels safe.

"I manage pretty well because I live within the bounds that I've established for myself," says Meg. "If I stay off of elevators, freeways, and don't drive too far from home. . . . I can keep my anxiety within manageable limits."[46]

Phobias are about avoidance. A man with a specific phobia keeps a wide distance between himself and what frightens him. A woman with a social phobia avoids social situations. A person with agoraphobia may avoid places or situations where her panic attacks have happened in the past. With agoraphobia, however, the list of places to avoid grows over time, and the person's world gets smaller and smaller. The constant fear of having a panic attack makes it very difficult to live a normal life.

"Because of the fear of having a panic attack, the list of places or situations to be avoided can grow to include wide-open areas, closed areas such as elevators, shopping malls, theaters, concerts, public transportation, being alone, and anywhere where there might be a crowd or the necessity of standing in line," Marshall says. "Not surprisingly, many agoraphobics are homebound, unable to work, and often completely dependent on others."[47]

Not only do agoraphobics come to feel trapped in their homes, but many also start to depend on a family member to stay at home with them. They may have panic attacks even when they are alone, and therefore, they not only feel trapped but they also depend completely on others. Agoraphobia is a disability, and living with it can be even harder than not being able to walk, for instance, or to see or hear. No assistive device like a hearing aid or a wheelchair exists that can make life easier for a person who fears everything. In fact, very few people know about agoraphobia or understand the condition. Even the agoraphobic person's friends and family may not understand. They might get frustrated and stop visiting, and this only makes things worse. Agoraphobics mostly live in a very small and very lonely world, too afraid to come out and make friends, and too afraid to get help.

Little Help for the Harried

Most people who have phobias admit their fears are not logical. They may wonder why they cannot just snap out of them, be brave, and move on. The question troubles both phobics and the therapists who try to treat them. Phobias are very frustrating things. Perhaps most frustrating of all is that the only way to get rid of a fear, it seems, is to face it.

"Phobias are difficult to treat because sufferers are slow to come for treatment and often afraid of confronting their fears when they get to treatment,"[48] says psychiatrist Gavin Andrews. Many phobics who dread this fear-facing treatment, the only known way to cure a phobia, choose to live in fear. For this reason, phobias may be a more widespread health problem than diseases such as diabetes or cancer.

Phobias can also be deadly. It is not that the fear itself kills anyone (although someone having a panic attack may, for a moment, feel like he is going to die). The true problem is that living in nonstop fear can make people very depressed, even suicidal. They may also turn to drugs or alcohol, hoping that such substances will help them dull their fear. The thing that sets off a person's phobia might not be a life-and-death situation, but the phobia itself could be. Therefore, it is essential to treat fear before it ruins someone's life.

CHAPTER FOUR

Treating a Phobia

Phobias, by definition, change lives. They are fears that slowly grow and eventually they affect a person's choices. When a fear of airplanes keeps a college student from going home for the holidays, or ruins a couple's honeymoon, or keeps a man from making it to the hospital for his dying mother's last hours, it causes serious problems. The person with the phobia might even start to look for answers and help.

However, getting help is not something that everyone with a phobia chooses to do. After all, a phobia can be embarrassing. Fears of heights, airplanes, or tight spaces may be common, but a fear of cotton balls or hard-boiled eggs is not. It might be more embarrassing to admit to the fear than to live with it, so many people choose to live with their fear.

Social phobias and agoraphobia are a different matter. While a fear of thunderstorms or poisonous snakes or even air travel does not necessarily make a normal life impossible, a phobia of using the telephone or of being farther than three blocks from home can soon start to affect a person's lifestyle. Social phobias and agoraphobia can take a huge toll on happiness and success.

"Since my divorce, I have had no life," says Marge, a woman who struggles with a social phobia. "I go to work and come home. I can't stand being with people, particularly if I have to meet new people, and men scare me to death."[49]

As with any psychological illness, which is what phobias are, the first step is admitting there is a problem—and often, it is a serious one. But because phobias are treated by psychiatrists and psychologists, people who specialize in mental disorders, needing to see one of these professionals can be embarrassing in itself. There is a social stigma about having a mental disorder and needing treatment for it. People with phobias do not want others to think they are crazy. This is one reason phobics tend to put off treatment for their problem.

It also does not help that phobias are poorly understood, even by the doctors who treat people who have them. The way doctors try to reach out to phobics, many of whom live silently with their fears, is not always helpful either. Psychiatrist John R. Marshall describes a day when he was a guest on a call-in radio program. He was sure that people listening at home would pick up the phone and tell him about their social fears, but nobody called. Marshall did not understand why.

"On the air, I remarked that I was surprised, and even a little disappointed, that most of the people who called in seemed to have anxiety-related disorders other than social phobia," Marshall says. "On my next day in the clinic, one of my socially phobic patients told me she had heard me on the radio. 'And if others are like me, there is no way you could have expected them to call in,'" she told him. "'I would never dream of calling in to a radio program. That would only multiply my chances of making a complete fool of myself—astronomically.'"[50]

Misunderstanding Phobias

Even Marshall, a doctor who has spent his career working with people who have phobias, did not really understand what it feels like to live with a phobia. Being misunderstood is one reason why some phobics live with their fear for a long time before they ask for help. They may not feel that even their doctors really understand what is bothering them, and they may be quite right.

Other patients with phobias avoid doctors because they have found a way to treat the problem themselves. They may have discovered that alcohol or drugs calm them down when they feel afraid or help them to loosen up in a crowd. Drug or alcohol addiction is common in people with phobias—much more

Some people with phobias attempt to manage their fears by consuming alcohol or drugs in order to feel less anxious.

so than in people who do not live in constant fear of something. Some researchers even think the typical alcoholic may actually be a social phobic who has learned to cover up the first problem with another—drinking. "Social phobics, more than patients with any other anxiety disorder, say that they use alcohol and certain drugs to relieve anxiety,"[51] says Marshall.

For a social phobic who also struggles with alcohol addiction, getting help for either problem is twice as hard. During Alcoholics Anonymous (AA) meetings, which are supposed to help people get over their addiction to drinking, people in the group take turns talking about themselves. Doing this while sober, which is required during such a meeting, is a nightmare for someone with a fear of speaking in public. Therefore, many phobics who drink heavily end up avoiding these kinds of meetings. They get little or no support, at least from social groups such as Alcoholics Anonymous, as they try to get rid of their addiction.

Doctors are realizing how important it is to help society understand phobias. If more phobics understood their fear and knew they could get help, perhaps more would turn to doctors and not to alcohol or drugs. Treating phobias early is very important, because the longer a person lives with a phobia, the worse it is likely to get. The worse it gets, the more it ruins someone's life. So doctors sometimes take a bold first step to treatment and prescribe medication to start beating a phobia before it gets out of hand.

Medication

Unfortunately, there is no medication that makes the symptoms of a phobia go away. When doctors prescribe medication for phobias, they are really just trying to reduce the person's fear response temporarily so that they can get at the root of the problem. In order to treat the underlying phobia, it is sometimes necessary to stop the panic response first, and medications that relax the person can help.

"When your anxiety level is very high, or when you've been avoiding situations for a long time," says author Edmund J. Bourne, "you may, quite literally, have difficulty 'getting out the door.'" These are the situations in which medication might be useful. "While not providing a long-term solution," Bourne says, "medication can sometimes help you get over the initial blocks and barriers to getting started."[52]

Medications are only part of the treatment for a phobia. There is not a pill that an arachnaphobic can take to prevent ever being afraid of spiders again. In fact, medications are rarely used at all in treating simple phobias, and they are only sometimes used as a starting point when treating social phobias and agoraphobia.

A medication is useful only if it stops a person's panic long enough for him or her to start treatment. After all, beating a

Phobia Medications

Some doctors prescribe medications to people who have phobias. This medication is usually antidepressants or antianxiety drugs.

Medications to treat depression also help some people react less strongly to fear. Since depression and phobias often go hand in hand, it makes sense to prescribe antidepressants, such as the drug Paxil, to people with phobias.

Unlike antidepressants, which are taken regularly, antianxiety drugs (called benzodiazepines) are usually taken only when phobics know they might be in a situation that they fear. A social phobic, for example, might take this medication if he has to go to a wedding or give a presentation at work.

Medications might help people live with their fear, but they do not cure it. Patients may even become dependent on their medication, and this could actually make their phobia worse.

It seems the only true way to get over a phobia is to face the fear—without taking medication.

phobia means facing and overcoming the fear itself, not just masking it with medication. Any phobic who wants to get better must go down the scary path of confronting his or her fear. One kind of treatment, called cognitive therapy, forces patients to take a critical first step, one that might even seem impossible for some phobics at the beginning of therapy. Cognitive treatments force phobics to think, in detail, about their fear.

Cognitive Therapy

For most people, the first step in getting over a phobia is to learn to be reasonable about it. People with phobias are far more afraid of some things than they logically should be. Understanding why this is will be important if they are ever to get over their fear.

During cognitive therapy for a phobia, a person practices thinking about fear more sensibly. She might make a list of things that worry her or things she is afraid will happen. Then her doctor or therapist helps her prove to herself that what she fears is mostly in her imagination. For example, consider Courtney, a student who is terrified that everyone in her class will stare at her and make fun of her if she walks in late. Courtney's doctor might tell her to pay close attention to what happens when other students walk in late. She might be relieved to find that the rest of the class hardly notices. She might then begin to realize that if *she* were to walk in late, the other students would react the same way—they would hardly notice. Realizing that the thing she fears is actually not very likely to happen could be an important step for Courtney in treating her phobia.

"In many cases," say psychologists Mark R. Leary and Robin M. Kowalski, "people's perceived self-presentation difficulties are more imagined than real. Socially anxious people also overestimate the degree to which their nervousness is apparent to other people."[53] For Courtney, realizing that her fear of being

A person with a phobia may seek the help of a cognitive therapist, who can help patients rationally examine the details of the things and situations they find fearful so that they can eventually overcome them.

judged is all in her head and that her classmates are not watching her nearly as closely as she thinks might be all she needs to start beating her phobia.

Many phobics, however, already understand that their fear is out of proportion to any actual threat. Cognitive therapy alone may not lead to a cure. Most phobics also need to practice exposing themselves to the thing they dread. This will prove to them that they can survive what they fear—and that it may not be as bad as they think after all.

Behavioral Therapy

Getting over a phobia, say Michelle G. Crasky and her colleagues in their book, *Mastering Your Fears and Phobias*, involves direct experience with the feared object or situation in order to learn that it is harmless. "Treatment may last as little as one session or as many as 10, depending on the type of phobia," they say. "In our experience, animal phobias, blood phobias, and injection phobias often take fewer sessions."[54] These researchers have found that patients who are afraid of heights or of situations such as driving, for example, tend to take longer to cure.

The theory behind behavioral therapy is that phobias are learned. The person who has a fearful reaction in a certain situation decides it is best to avoid that situation in the future. The more he avoids it, the more he trains himself to be afraid of it. Psychiatrists think that if phobics can learn their fear this way, then they can also unlearn it. The trick is the right approach, one that does not require the person to face too much of the fear too fast.

During behavioral therapy, phobics face their fears head-on, but they do this slowly. Exposure to the thing that frightens them happens in small doses at first, depending on how much fright they can handle. Behavioral therapy is a series of baby steps toward beating a phobia. "Simply visualizing the feared object or activity might be enough to trigger the patient's fear at first," journalist Susan Stevens says. "Then therapy might involve looking at pictures or even virtual reality experiences until the patient can cope with the real thing."[55]

A person receiving behavioral therapy to treat his fear of fish, for example, might first spend time reading books about fish and studying pictures of them. In the beginning, even this might be enough to frighten him, but later in therapy, he might work up to visiting an aquarium and looking at real, living fish. Eventually, he might move on to actually touching a fish, then wading in a pool of water with a fish. By the end of therapy, he still might not *like* fish, but the hope is that he will be able to be near fish—to walk into a doctor's office that has an aquarium in the waiting room, for example—and not launch into full-blown panic.

Some people overcome their phobias through behavioral therapy, during which they expose themselves to the things they fear a little at a time. A person who fears fish, for example, may eventually visit an aquarium as part of behavioral therapy.

"It is helpful to confront the behaviors that one avoids, since doing more of what is feared often, though not always, tends to reduce anxiety,"[56] says Marshall. Behavioral therapy is thought to be the best treatment for specific phobias—as long as the patient can work up the courage to go through with it.

Social phobias tend to be more complicated fears, so behavioral therapy treatments usually take longer and are more difficult. Still, behavioral therapy can be helpful for patients with social phobias. The key is always to start small. During behavioral therapy, a social phobic must set simple goals she feels she can meet. Then she works up to larger goals—perhaps even delivering a speech to a crowd.

Overcoming a fear of public speaking is one of the best-known uses of behavioral therapy. Because stage fright is such a common fear, many different programs and classes are offered to help people put this life-changing problem behind them and face a positive future. J. Lyman Macinnis, author of *The Elements of Great Public Speaking*, believes that exposure

A person with a fear of public speaking may practice giving a speech to a small group as part of her effort to overcome her fear.

to this fear, beginning with talking to small groups and moving to larger crowds, is the only way to beat it. "Many people would list public speaking ahead of dying on a list of things they dread most," Macinnis says. "Early on you need to remember that you will eventually overcome your fear as you gain experience."[57]

Even agoraphobics, whose fears include not only public speaking but also just about everything outside of their comfort zone, can take part in behavioral therapy. They might work up to leaving their home, then walking one block from home, then two blocks. In time, they may be able to visit a few places, such as the supermarket, without panicking.

In order to get treatment of any kind, however, a phobic must first do two things: Admit the problem is serious enough to get help for it, and then work up the courage to actually get help. Reaching out for help is a tall order for many people with the kind of crippling fear a phobia can cause. Getting treatment for the problem is easier said than done.

Obstacles to Treatment

Not everyone with a phobia likes to think of it as a medical problem. A person who is already embarrassed because of a fear most people would find ridiculous might be even more humiliated to head to the nearest psychiatrist for advice. Even phobics who do think they have a mental problem might be too busy avoiding frightening things to bother with treatment. Agoraphobes, especially, often worry that they are going crazy when they have a panic attack—but visiting a psychiatrist might set off a panic attack, too. So they may reason it is safer just to stay home.

It might help if science could track down what exactly causes some people to develop phobias while others do not. Not all people who have been bitten by a dog or stung by a bee, for example, develop a fear of dogs or bees, and not all people with dog or bee phobias have been bitten or stung, either. Where phobias come from still puzzles scientists, and therefore, no hard and fast cure for them exists.

Phobias Affect the Ecosystem

Snakes are the object of a very common phobia. The silent slither-
ers are among the most feared and hated creatures on the planet.
Although few snake species pose any real danger to people, many
a serpent has been a victim of the "kill first, ask questions later"
approach.

Snake species around the world are becoming endangered. While
this may sound like good news to ophidiophobes (people who fear
snakes), it is a tragedy for the planet. Snakes have an important
place in the ecosystem, but like many other animals, their habitats
are being overtaken by humans. Unfortunately, not nearly as many
people stand up for snakes as for fuzzier critters like pandas. Quite
the contrary, even though king cobras are endangered, fear makes
people hunt them down and kill them instead of protecting them.
(The fact that this snake can
drop a full-grown elephant with
one venomous bite does not
help its situation.)

Phobias have nothing to do
with logic or common sense,
and neither does the senseless
killing of animals just because
they look creepy.

The reputation of some animals
that are highly feared, such as
the king cobra, has led to people
killing them indiscriminately, even
when the threat of danger is low.

"There are effective treatments for panic disorder and the phobias," says psychiatrist Gavin Andrews. "The problem is that few people with these disorders attend for treatment and, when they do, few are treated appropriately."[58]

Treatment for the same phobia may also differ from person to person. Doctors have discovered that what works for one phobic might not work at all for another. This is just one of the challenges of treating them.

The symptoms of phobias can also be hard to spot. There is no rash or fever or blood test that identifies a phobia. Most people with a specific phobia know that they have it (it is pretty clear because they panic in the presence of spiders, clowns, or something else they can easily identify). People with social phobias and agoraphobia, on the other hand, usually live with much broader fears and may just think they are horribly shy, unsocial, or even mentally unstable people. "Many undiagnosed victims suffer silently, not understanding their painful and limiting disability,"[59] says H. Michael Zal, author of *Panic Disorder: The Great Pretender*.

Educating the public about phobias, especially social phobias and agoraphobias, is one way to get through to the many people who live with one and do not realize it. Doctors, too, need to understand more about phobias. Unless they specialize in treating fears, many doctors might miss the symptoms of a phobia in a patient who comes in for something else. An agoraphobic, for example, might go to his doctor because his heart was racing and he was gasping for breath and he thinks he had a heart attack. The doctor might rule out a heart attack, but unless she has experience with phobias, she might send the man home without diagnosing the fear that is causing all the trouble. Alcoholics or drug addicts, too, may never be recognized as the phobics they truly are, and they may suffer through different treatment programs while never getting help for the fear that is actually the problem.

People with a specific phobia of doctors, meanwhile, not only avoid seeking treatment for their phobia, but they also probably avoid getting treated for everything else as well. A person with a phobia of doctors may avoid all kinds of important tests and procedures, including flu shots, cancer screenings, and teeth cleanings. She may become so unhealthy over the years that panic is the least of her worries. Medical researchers have no clear idea how many individuals struggle with this kind of phobia, precisely because a doctor is the last person any of them would ever tell about it. Researchers do know, however, that phobias of all kinds affect a significant percentage of the population. With so many people living in fear, phobias have widespread effects, not just for the people who suffer with them but for society as a whole.

The Cost of Phobias

Social phobias and agoraphobia often set in or get worse during a person's teenage years. The boy seated in the back row of the classroom with the hood of his sweatshirt pulled over his head might never talk to anyone. He might refuse to raise his hand or answer questions, and he might get low grades because he will not give any presentations in front of the class under any circumstances. He might start to miss a lot of school, and one day, he might stop coming to school altogether.

The student's problem could be a social phobia that nobody recognized. Now he is a high school dropout and feels no hope of furthering his education or even getting a good job. After all, he would never make it through a job interview.

This scenario could be more common than anyone realizes. Untreated phobias have big costs, both to individuals and to society. As people suffer with their fear in silence, they miss out on educational opportunities. They may even live on welfare because of a phobia that makes them too afraid to get and keep a job.

"The phobias make a significant contribution to the burden of disease,"[60] says Andrews. He claims that phobias have the same impact on our society as diabetes and colon cancer. It is unknown how many brilliant students have dropped out of school because of a social phobia, for instance, and this could be having widespread effects on society. A phobic's condition

Phobias can be at the root of some students' academic and social problems, making it difficult for them to stay in school.

may not be physically painful, but it is painfully frustrating, and phobias deserve the same kind of attention that other illnesses receive.

Depression is one major social problem that is tied to phobias. One-third or more of people living with a phobia have also suffered from depression. For people with social phobias or agoraphobia, nearly half have suffered from depression. It is not difficult to understand why living with a significant fear of people or places could lead to loneliness and depression. Many social phobics and agoraphobics have few, if any, friends—not because they do not want and need friendship, but because their fear gets in the way. They may seem grumpy and unpleasant to others, while inside they might be desperate to have a friend.

"I am pushing all my friends away," says one phobic who also struggles with depression. "I just do not want to go out at all. I'd rather be home by myself or in bed and avoid the world. And then I feel lonely."[61]

Phobias might not be widely recognized as a true or major illness, but depression certainly is. Doctors have been trying for years to educate people about depression and its consequences. Television commercials and advertisements in magazines and on billboards educate the public about the symptoms of depression and about the medications that exist that can ease those symptoms. Phobics are especially in need of this information. They are shockingly high on the list of depressed people who are likely to attempt suicide. One social phobic who dropped out of high school describes how deeply depression about her phobia affects her: "I have been working on a highway crew. This is not where I wanted to be in my life. . . . I think about suicide all the time."[62]

Unfortunately, depression can mask the very phobia that is causing it. Getting help for the depression alone stops short of treating the real problem. Medication and therapy do not always work to get rid of a phobic's deepest fears, and many phobics live with their fear and never seek therapy at all.

Phobias have been around for thousands of years, and despite major advances in medicine, phobias still affect as many as one in every three people worldwide. Historically, there has been little help for people who suffer from irrational fears. Modern technology, however, might finally be able to provide the help that phobics need.

CHAPTER FIVE

Phobias and Technology

A young woman stands on the roof of a fifty-story building. She clutches the handrail so hard her knuckles are white. Her heart is pounding. Her T-shirt has big circles of sweat under the arms. But she takes a deep breath and looks over the edge.

There are two people watching, but they do not seem at all concerned that the woman might fall. After all, it is actually a very short distance to the ground. The woman is in her eighth and final session of virtual reality therapy, or VRT, to treat her fear of heights. And although she still feels uncomfortable, the therapy has given her the courage to stand on top of a virtual building without panicking.

When the researchers turn off the simulation, the woman has both feet planted on the floor of the room. She takes off her virtual reality helmet and gives them a shaky smile—"I did it."

In just a few weeks, she progressed from the first session, in which the program created the illusion that she was standing on a very low bridge, through sessions that involved higher and higher simulated places until she had the courage to face the sensation of being fifty stories in the air. She is sweaty, her heart is racing, but now she knows she can stand in a very high place and live to tell about it.

Virtual therapy is being used to treat all kinds of phobias, from fears of heights or small spaces to fears of giving a speech or driving a car. Computer technology can create an illusion, or fake environment, of almost any kind of situation that frightens people. VRT is behavioral therapy in the extreme, but because it is not a real situation, just a very convincing illusion, more and more phobics are finding they have the courage to go through virtual reality treatment for their problem.

"VRT can overcome some of the difficulties inherent in the traditional treatment of phobias," say VRT pioneers Max M. North, Sarah M. North, and Joseph R. Coble. "VRT can provide stimuli for patients who have difficulty imagining fear-producing triggers and/or are too phobic to undergo real-life experiences in public."[63]

VRT makes it possible for people with all sorts of different phobias to overcome their fears more safely and more privately than ever before. Knowing they might be able to face their problems virtually, at their own pace, without being stared at or laughed at by anyone else, has finally made treatment possible for phobic people who could never face it before.

Virtually Beating Fear

At VRT clinics such as the Virtual Reality Medical Center in San Diego, California, patients wear special helmets with TV screens and earphones that make them feel they are in a particular place. Everything they see and hear seems completely real to them. They can experience the very situations that they are most afraid of, but the whole time they are in the therapist's office. They can stop the simulation at any moment.

"For me, because of the nature of the feedback I received during the VRT sessions, I was able to identify my 'flying rough spots' easier," says Kathy Feldman, who claims that her fear of airline travel was so strong before virtual therapy that she once abandoned her own children on an airplane when she lost her courage to go through with her flight and sprinted back to the airport terminal. "Virtual Reality Therapy gave me more concrete feedback about what I, as a nervous flyer, needed to work through to begin flying again."[64]

Virtual reality technology helps people get over fears of everything from thunderstorms to needles. It is proving especially helpful for people who want to face fears of things such as tornadoes, which do not occur in times and places that are predictable or convenient for a treatment schedule. Based on the idea of behavioral therapy, which exposes patients to what they fear and builds up to more and more frightening situations, VRT sessions make it easy to start small and move to higher goals.

During VRT, a person who has a phobia of spiders might begin with a session in which the VRT helmet shows a spider across the room. The next session might show a spider in a closed jar. In the third session, the jar might be open. Slowly, the patient might build up to the point where he can actually touch the spider, at least in the virtual reality world.

A man demonstrates virtual reality technology that people with phobias can use as part of their therapy, allowing them to simulate an experience with something they are fearful of in a controlled environment.

The progess patients make in virtual reality treatment also carries over to the real world. Logically, the phobic patient undergoing VRT knows the whole time that he can just take off the helmet and the virtual spider will go away. However, one of the defining characteristics of phobias is that they are not logical. North and his colleagues have found that VRT experiences do cause the same feelings of panic as real-life behavioral therapy sessions do, even though the person realizes the spider or other feared thing is not really there. Thus, virtual behavioral therapy allows patients to experience the thing they fear just as if they were exposed to it in the real world.

"When subjected to virtual phobic-invoking situations, participants exhibited the same types of responses as would be exhibited in real-world situations," they say. "These responses included anxiety, avoidance, and physical symptoms."[65] Basically, people who have a phobia in the real world also have a phobia in the virtual world. Many patients who make it through a VRT program, therefore, find that they are able to start facing their fears even outside the therapy setting.

North and his colleagues describe one patient who finished a VRT program to get rid of her fear of flying. By the end of her sessions, she faced the treatments with much less fear than she had in the beginning. But the researchers wanted to test how well she would respond if she actually took to the air.

"She was flown, in the company of the therapist, in a helicopter for approximately 10 minutes at low altitude over a beach on the Gulf of Mexico," they say. "As with the VRT sessions, she reported some anxiety at the beginning but rapidly grew more comfortable. Now the subject comfortably flies for long distances and experiences much less anxiety."[66]

A high-tech helmet and a special computer program can do wonders for people with specific phobias, who can pinpoint exactly what frightens them and just how much of it they can handle before panicking. Scientists have found that virtual technology can also help people with a fear of less specific things, such as public humiliation or having a panic attack.

Just What the Doctor Ordered

If you have a phobia, your doctor might tell you to spend time playing video games.

The same thing that makes some games so much fun to play makes them great for helping people get over their phobias. Graphics are more realistic than ever before, and some games have software to let you build your own graphic environment. In 2003 Canadian researchers decided to try exposing people to their phobias using two popular video games that let you create your own realistic situations on screen: Half-Life and Unreal Tournament.

Patients playing Half-Life were exposed to on-screen, spiderlike aliens to help them deal with their phobia of eight-legged things. Patients playing Unreal Tournament, meanwhile, were dealing with fears of heights and small spaces by creating these kinds of situations in the game. Patients who played these games made some progress in getting over their phobias.

The bottom line? Some video games might actually be good for you—especially if you have a phobia.

VRT for Social Phobias

People who fear public speaking can take part in a program that simulates a real auditorium filled with people. The patient practices giving a speech to the virtual room and gets a sense of what it feels like to talk to a large group. A virtual auditorium created at Clark Atlanta University in Georgia includes everything from a wooden podium to an audience of one hundred people—all virtual, of course. An amplifier with direct connection to the virtual reality software and hardware even allows patients to "hear the echo of their voices," say North and colleagues. After treatment in this virtual environment, several previously phobic patients "can comfortably speak in front of a crowd with better confidence."[67]

There are programs for agoraphobics, too. Using virtual reality, they can practice being in any number of situations that would normally frighten them: a dark room, a crowded theater, an empty beach, a subway train. The hope is that by exposing themselves to situations that scare them, without being around real people who might laugh, point, and make a panic attack even worse, social phobics and agoraphobics can begin to break through their fear. When they realize they can survive a situation they once thought might kill them, they slowly become able to practice the same kinds of activities in the real world.

"Virtual reality therapy appears to be very effective in reducing self-reported anxiety,"[68] say North and colleagues. VRT treatments, they say, reduce anxiety and are helping people to face all kinds of frightening situations.

Techno-Tools for Phobics

In a high-tech world where people can pretend to touch snakes and spiders, stand on tall buildings, or give speeches to rooms full of fake people, phobics can also get help with day-to-day experiences that are challenging for them. After all, people who have phobias struggle with peculiar hardships. Some avoid all forms of transportation, for example, because they fear that once inside a car, a bus, or a train, a panic attack will make them scramble for the nearest door or open window. People with this kind of a phobia might feel forced to live within walking distance of everything they need, such as their job and their grocery store.

Other phobics never finish high school or never go to college because they are so worried about what their teachers and classmates think of them that attending class actually makes them ill. Still other phobics live the life of shut-ins, hermits who are too afraid to step outside the safety of their own home. For any of these people and millions more, a computer might be their best and only friend. These days, computers and the Internet make it possible for many people with phobias to live fairly normal lives right from the safety of their home.

Computer technology can allow people with social phobias access to the outside world that they otherwise would not have because of their fears, enabling them to interact socially and professionally with others from the comfort of their homes.

A personal computer and an Internet connection let people with a phobia of telephones "chat" with friends while never having to pick up a phone, for example. The same equipment makes it possible for people with social phobias to earn advanced degrees by taking classes entirely online. More professions than ever allow people to work from home, allowing them to avoid a dreaded commute to work. For people whose phobias trap them indoors, technology makes it possible to work, play, and survive.

Psychologists Virginia Smith Harvey and Janet F. Carlson say computers can be very useful tools for people who have anxiety and phobias. For one thing, they explain, computers allow patients "to establish on-line support groups that provide opportunities for individuals to network with others who experience similar issues."[69]

However, not everyone agrees that forming a dependence on technology is the right way to go about coping with a phobia. Left untreated, a phobia of one thing may lead to more kinds of phobias. Someone who starts out shy as a teenager may turn into a young adult with a social phobia, and then a middle-aged adult afraid of leaving home. This is even more likely to happen if the shy teenager is never forced to spend time around other people. Harvey and Carlson agree that using computers as an excuse to avoid all social interaction can make certain kinds of phobias worse. "The loss of face-to-face contact can be a serious issue,"[70] they say.

Society-Wide Phobias

Salem, Massachusetts, was a scary place to be in 1692. The early American colony accused, jailed, and prosecuted two hundred of its citizens, because they were believed to be witches.

In what came to be known as the Salem Witch Trials, people gave courtroom testimony that was largely based on stories of dreams and visions. Twenty people were executed even though there was no hard evidence that they had done anything wrong. There are many theories as to why an entire colony grew hysterical about witches in its midst, but this early American epidemic of witch phobia remains as puzzling and senseless as any other irrational fear.

Could this kind of society-wide phobia happen again? Some people worry that fear of terrorists could lead to a similar kind of persecution and abuse today.

Fear of witchcraft and evil was at the core of the Salem Witch Trials in Massachusetts during the 1690s, during which 200 people were put on trial and 20 put to death.

Some researchers, such as Bernardo J. Carducci, director of the Shyness Research Institute in New Albany, Indiana, worry that technology may even be breeding social phobias. "It is having an effect," Carducci says. "Think about it. Children don't see people interacting as much. Children come home and get on their computers. That means social isolation and a loss in negotiation."[71]

These days, people do their banking at ATMs, scan their own groceries at self-checkout stations, and shop online. Coffee shops are quieter as people sip while surfing the Internet using a wireless connection. Almost everyone owns a cell phone, but even then, more people these days seem to be texting than actually talking. It is even becoming common for people to date through their computers.

Thus, at the same time technology is helping people who have phobias, it is also making it easier for people to avoid seeking treatment. With the Internet, phobics can now get through life without ever having to get over their panic attacks or form real, face-to-face relationships with other people. It is possible that technology is making social phobias a greater problem than they have ever been in the past.

Technophobes

There is also evidence that technology itself is becoming the object of some people's phobias. If a suspicious-looking package with wires and batteries attached to it turns up outside a school or a government building, for instance, people retreat to the other side of the street and call police to report a possible bomb threat. This is a typical response to a fairly new source of phobias—technological things.

"Anything with wires and batteries is automatically suspect," says technology writer Andrew Kantor. "There are far more benign things with wires and batteries than dangerous ones. But try telling that to people who view all things technological with suspicion."[72]

Phobias thrive on technology in other ways, too. These days anyone can watch a video of practically anything online.

The vast amount of information available online, some of it graphic and alarming, may cause people to develop phobias of situations that are otherwise not a part of their daily lives.

People who watch violent or disturbing scenes in streaming Web videos may develop phobias of things that are not at all likely to happen to them.

"People have shifted their phobias to obscure and distant threats—things like global climate change, alien invasions, and secondhand smoking," says economist and public policy researcher Stephen Moore. "What else do we worry about? War? Floods and tornadoes? AIDS? Nuclear accidents? Drunk drivers? Acts of terrorism? Your newborn infant dying in the middle of the night from sudden infant death syndrome? Believe it or not, the death rate from every single one of these menaces is down—in most cases way down."[73]

Phobias, however, have always had more to do with imagination than logic. Many phobias, especially specific ones, start when the person witnesses something terrible, and more than ever, video footage lets anyone be a "witness" to any number of terrible things. A person who has never experienced an earthquake or a tornado used to have little reason to fear one. But now that television can show us how frightening these natural phenomena can be, the number of people who fear them has risen. This is how technology creates phobias even as it helps some people to battle them.

"Americans fear levels of crime that do not exist, even when actual crime rates are falling, because of media portrayals," says phobia researcher Peter N. Stearns. "They worry about child abduction or teenage gambling when both are extremely rare, again because journalists so often tell them that youth are at far greater risk than adults realize. . . . They make huge mistakes about the likelihood of certain feared diseases."[74]

Not Just Bugs and Heights Anymore

Since the terrorist attacks on September 11, 2001, in the United States, the fear of terrorist attacks has risen to one of the top twenty things Americans are most afraid of. Other new phobias that did not exist a century ago include drive-by shootings, AIDS, and nuclear war.

What people have feared throughout history has always been related to the kind of world they live in. If anyone had taken a fear survey during the Middle Ages, when the bubonic plague wiped out one-third of the population of Europe, it is likely that this disease easily would have topped the phobias list. In today's phobia surveys, no one mentions bubonic plague, but leukemia, the avian bird flu, and sudden infant death syndrome (SIDS) pop up repeatedly.

Phobias throughout history are often tied to the events of the day. The September 11, 2001, attacks on the World Trade Center and the Pentagon, for example, ushered in an increase in the fear of terrorism among Americans.

Phobias of snakes, bees, heights, and cramped places have been persistent through time, but not all fears have this kind of staying power. Some superstitions and beliefs that once led to phobias have become outdated. Old fears now thought of as silly have simply been replaced with fears of modern threats. In Scotland in the 1500s, for example, King James I had a phobia of unsheathed swords. Perhaps if he had lived today, he would fear unholstered guns. It seems fears themselves do not ever really vanish. They merely change with changing times. The world may be safer in many ways than ever before, but people continue to suffer from life-altering, irrational phobias. There will always be something to dread.

Forever Fear?

Fear is deeply and permanently rooted in the human experience. All of us are biologically programmed to feel it. For thrill seekers, it gives spice to life. For people in dangerous situations, it can be life saving. For phobics, it can be a crippling, isolating enemy. Fear has puzzled scientists and medical experts for more than two millennia. As with so many other secrets buried deep in the mind, the answers to how this natural and usually useful sensation can go so wrong in some people may never be found. Phobias have always been part of the human experience, and they might always be.

Notes

Chapter 1: What Is a Phobia?

1. Edmund J. Bourne, *The Anxiety and Phobia Workbook*, 4th ed. Oakland, CA: New Harbinger, 2005, p. 47.
2. Lynne L. Hall, "Fighting Phobias: The Things That Go Bump in the Mind," FDA Consumer, March 1997, p. 12.
3. Quoted in Jeffrey Slonim, "The Horror," *Artforum International*, April 1994, p. 11.
4. Quoted in Slonim, "The Horror," p. 11.
5. Quoted in *USA Today* (magazine), "Severe Weather Fears Can Be Debilitating," *USA Today*, December 1996, p. 8.
6. Quoted in "Living in Fear: Wendy Sloane Talks to Five People Struggling with Fears That Reduce Them to Quivering Wrecks," *Sunday Mirror*, February 1, 1998.
7. Quoted in Hall, "Fighting Phobias," p. 12.
8. Thomas G. Plante, *Contemporary Clinical Psychology*, 2nd ed. Hoboken, NJ: Wiley, 1997, p. 165.
9. Bourne, *The Anxiety and Phobia Workbook*, p. 11.
10. Bourne, *The Anxiety and Phobia Workbook*, p. 11.
11. Bourne, *The Anxiety and Phobia Workbook*, p. 12.
12. Raeann Dumont, *The Sky Is Falling: Understanding and Coping with Phobias, Panic, and Obsessive-Compulsive Disorders*. New York: Norton, 1995, p. 60.
13. Lisa Capps and Elinor Ochs, *Constructing Panic: The Discourse of Agoraphobia*. Cambridge, MA: Harvard University Press, 1997, p. 3.

Chapter 2: Who Gets Phobias?

14. Helen Saul, *Phobias: Fighting the Fear*. New York: Arcade, 2004, p. 11.
15. Saul, *Phobias*, p. 164.

16. Madeleine Brindley, "Fears and Phobias That Can Spiral Out of Control," *Western Mail* (Wales newspaper), April 9, 2007.
17. Brindley, "Fears and Phobias."
18. Bourne, *The Anxiety and Phobia Workbook*, p. 12.
19. Quoted in Mary Keenan and Tessa Cunningham, "Phobias: Why the Everyday World Terrifies Us," *Mirror*, April 11, 1998.
20. Quoted in Keenan and Cunningham, "Phobias."
21. Aaron T. Beck and Gary Emery, *Anxiety Disorders and Phobias: A Common Perspective.* New York: BasicBooks, 1985, p. 124.
22. Hall, "Fighting Phobias," p. 12.
23. John R. Marshall, *Social Phobia: From Shyness to Stage Fright.* New York: BasicBooks, 1994, p. 222.
24. Hall, "Fighting Phobias," p. 13.
25. Quoted in Lucy Elkins, "Don't Panic (It's Only a Fish!)," *Daily Mail*, April 17, 2007.
26. Quoted in Keenan and Cunningham, "Phobias."
27. Saul, *Phobias*, p. 50.
28. Quoted in Elkins, "Don't Panic."
29. Saul, *Phobias*, p. 59.

Chapter 3: Living with a Phobia

30. Quoted in Keenan and Cunningham, "Phobias."
31. Quoted in Keenan and Cunningham, "Phobias."
32. Susan Stevens, "Face Your Fears: Conquering Phobias Requires Marshaling Your Brain's Cognitive Power," *Daily Herald*, October 25, 2004.
33. Stevens, "Face Your Fears."
34. Quoted in Keenan and Cunningham, "Phobias."
35. Stevens, "Face Your Fears."
36. Quoted in Marshall, *Social Phobia*, p. 2.
37. Saul, *Phobias*, p. 159.
38. Marshall, *Social Phobia*, p. 7.
39. Quoted in Marshall, *Social Phobia*, p. 7.

40. Marshall, *Social Phobia*, p. 18.
41. Marshall, *Social Phobia*, p. 35.
42. Marshall, *Social Phobia*, p. 36.
43. Quoted in Capps and Ochs, *Constructing Panic*, p. 17.
44. Capps and Ochs, *Constructing Panic*, p. 22.
45. Capps and Ochs, *Constructing Panic*, p. 22.
46. Quoted in Capps and Ochs, *Constructing Panic*, p. 17.
47. Marshall, *Social Phobia*, p. 195.
48. Gavin Andrews, "Epidemiology of Phobias: A Review," in *Phobias*, eds. Mario Maj, Hagop S. Akiskal, Juan José López-Ibor, and Ahmed Okasha. Hoboken, NJ: Wiley, 2004, p. 77.

Chapter 4: Treating a Phobia

49. Quoted in Marshall, *Social Phobia*, p. 168.
50. Marshall, *Social Phobia*, p. 30.
51. Marshall, *Social Phobia*, p. 152.
52. Bourne, *The Anxiety and Phobia Workbook*, p. 157.
53. Mark R. Leary and Robin M. Kowalski, "The Self-Presentation Model of Social Phobia," in *Social Phobia: Diagnosis, Assessment, and Treatment*, eds. Richard C. Heimberg, Michael R. Leibowitz, Debra A. Hope, and Franklin R. Schneier. New York: Guilford, 1995, p. 104.
54. Michelle G. Crasky, Martin M. Antony, and David H. Barlow, *Mastering Your Fears and Phobias: Therapist Guide*, 2nd ed. New York: Oxford University, Press, 2006, p. 100.
55. Stevens, "Face Your Fears."
56. Marshall, *Social Phobia*, p. 173.
57. J. Lyman Macinnis, *The Elements of Great Public Speaking: How to Be Calm, Confident, and Compelling*. Berkeley, CA: Ten Speed Press, 2006, pp. 12–13.
58. Andrews, "Epidemiology of Phobias," p. 75.
59. H. Michael Zal, *Panic Disorder: The Great Pretender*. Cambridge, MA: Perseus, 1990, p. 77.
60. Andrews, "Epidemiology of Phobias," p. 76.

61. Quoted in Depression Forums, www.depressionforums .org/forums/Depression-Social-Phobia-t9897. html&mode=threaded&pid=401025 (accessed April 15, 2008).

62. Quoted in Marshall, *Social Phobia*, p. 43.

Chapter 5: Phobias and Technology

63. Max M. North, Sarah M. North, and Joseph R. Coble, "Virtual Reality Therapy: An Effective Treatment for Psychological Disorders," in *Handbook of Virtual Environments: Design, Implementation, and Applications*, ed. Kay M. Stanney. Mahwah, NJ: Lawrence Erlbaum Associates, 2002, p. 1065.

64. Kathy Feldman, "Virtual Reality Therapy and How It Helped," Virtual Reality Medical Center, www.vrphobia .com/Feldman.htm (accessed April 15, 2008).

65. North, North, and Coble, "Virtual Reality Therapy," p. 1073.

66. North, North, and Coble, "Virtual Reality Therapy," p. 1066.

67. North, North, and Coble, "Virtual Reality Therapy," p. 1062.

68. North, North, and Coble, "Virtual Reality Therapy," p. 1069.

69. Virginia Smith Harvey and Janet F. Carlson, "Ethical and Professional Issues with Computer-Related Technology," *School Psychology Review* 32, 2003, p. 1.

70. Harvey and Carlson, "Ethical and Professional Issues," p. 1.

71. Quoted in Karen Goldberg Goff, "Nurturing a Shrinking Violet," *Washington Times*, March 18, 2001.

72. Andrew Kantor, "Silly Fear of Technology Must Be Overcome," *USA Today*, February 16, 2007, www.usatoday. com/tech/columnist/andrewkantor/2007-02-16-tech-fear _x.htm.

73. Stephen Moore, "Worried to Death," *American Enterprise* 10, no. 5, 1999, p. 9.
74. Peter N. Stearns, "Fear and Contemporary History: A Review Essay," *Journal of Social History* 40, no. 2, 2006, p. 477.

Glossary

acrophobia: Fear of heights.

agoraphobia: Fear of panicking in unfamiliar situations or places.

antianxiety drug: Medication that reduces feelings of stress, worry, or anxiety.

antidepressant: Medication to help with the symptoms of chronic, severe sadness.

anxiety: Feelings of intense fear or worry about an event or situation.

arachnophobia: Fear of spiders.

behavior therapy: A method of treating phobias by changing the patient's reactions to the feared object or situation.

cognitive therapy: A method of treating phobias by changing the negative thoughts the patient has about the feared object or situation.

cynophobia: Fear of dogs.

depression: A deep, lasting feeling of sadness and hopelessness.

ichthyophobia: Fear of fish.

leporiphobia: Fear of rabbits.

ophidiophobia: Fear of snakes.

panic: Sudden, overpowering feeling of terror, usually marked by sweating, shortness of breath, racing heart, and a need to escape.

phobia: A strong, illogical fear of an object or situation.

phobic: A person who has a phobia.

scoleciphobia: Fear of worms.

simple phobia: See *specific phobia*.

social phobia: Strong, lasting fear of one or more social situations or of being judged by others.

specific phobia: Strong, lasting fear of a particular object, animal, or situation.

virtual reality therapy: The use of virtual reality technology, or artificial environments created by computers, to treat phobias and other disorders.

Organizations to Contact

Anxiety Disorders Association of America (ADAA)

11900 Parklawn Drive, Suite 100
Rockville, MD 20852
(301) 231-9350
Fax: (301) 231-7392
www.adaa.org

Anxiety Disorders Association of America is a national network, founded in 1980 to promote the health of people with phobias and other anxiety disorders. It publishes the newsletter, *ADAA Reporter*.

Mental Health America

2000 N. Beauregard Street, 6th Floor
Alexandria, Virginia 22311
(800) 969-6642
Fax: (703) 684-5968
www.nmha.org

Mental Health America is a leading national nonprofit mental health organization in the United States. Its goal is to provide information about public health and help people find resources, research, and services to deal with mental problems including anxiety and phobias.

National Institute of Mental Health (NIMH)

Science Writing, Press, and Dissemination Branch
6001 Executive Boulevard, Room 8184, MSC 9663
Bethesda, MD 20892
(866) 615-6464
Fax: (301) 443-4279
nimhinfo@nih.gov
www.nimh.nih.gov

The world's largest scientific organization dedicated to mental health, the National Institute of Mental Health has information, resources, and research for a wide variety of mental conditions, including anxiety and phobias.

UCLA Semel Institute Anxiety Disorders Program

760 Westwood Plaza
Los Angeles, CA 90024
(310) 206-5133
www.semel.ucla.edu/adc

A research facility at the University of California, Los Angeles, the Semel Institute provides one of the finest programs in the United States for the study and treatment of anxiety disorders and phobias.

For Further Reading

Books

Shawn Allen, *Wish I Could Be There: Notes from a Phobic Life.* New York: Viking, 2007. This biography gives readers a close look at one person's phobic life and how fear creates serious boundaries.

Linda Manassee Buell, *Panic and Anxiety Disorder: 121 Tips, Real-Life Advice, Resources and More.* Poway, CA: Simplify Life, 2003. A selected resource of the Anxiety Disorders Association of America, this self-help book describes panic disorders such as phobias and different ways for sufferers to cope.

Ronald M. Doctor and Ada P. Kahn, *The Encyclopedia of Phobias, Fears, and Anxieties.* New York: Facts On File, 2008. This encyclopedia, explaining more than two thousand different phobias and stress causers, is a great place to look up anything from the fear of bees to the fear of knees.

Donald R. Gallo, ed., *What Are You Afraid Of? Stories About Phobias.* Cambridge, MA: Candlewick Press, 2007. This collection of short stories about people with phobias features ten different tales of what life is like under the burden of a crippling fear.

Internet Sources

Susan Donaldson James, "Not So Vain: Carly Simon's Panicky Past—Singer's Comeback Puts Past Struggles with Anxiety to the Test," *ABC News*, April 30, 2008, http://abcnews. go.com/Health/MindMoodNews/Story?id=4754440&page=1.

Jeffrey Kluger, "Fear Not!" *Time*, April 2, 2001, www.time.com/ time/magazine/article/0,9171,999584-1,00.html.

Richard Morris, "Famous People and Their Fears: Who Shares Your Phobia?" *Associated Content*, March 16, 2007, www. associatedcontent.com/article/166773/famous_people_and_ their_fears_who_shares.html?cat=2.

John Roach, "Friday the 13th Phobia Rooted in Ancient History," *National Geographic News*, August 12, 2004, http:// news.nationalgeographic.com/news/2004/02/0212_040212_ friday13.html.

Web Sites

DiscoveryHealth (www.discoveryhealth.com). This Web site provides an overview of phobias; treatments, including virtual therapy; and a "What's Your Phobia" interactive quiz.

The Phobia List (http://phobialist.com). Look up almost any fear you can think of on this alphabetized, online list of hundreds of phobias. You can also order a Phobias List poster and find links to helpful sites for phobics.

Index

Picture Credits

Cover: Image copyright Sean Nel, 2008. Used under license
    from Shutterstock.com
AP Images, 74, 83
Peter Bowater/Photo Researchers, Inc., 12
Image copyright George Burba, 2008. Used under license
    from Shutterstock.com, 63
Corbis/PunchStock, 48
David Gifford/Photo Researchers Inc., 51
© Digital Vision/Alamy, 33, 52
Getty Images, 10
Hans Neleman/Stone/Getty Images, 34
© iStockphoto.com/Clint Spencer, 21
© iStockphoto.com/blueclue, 58
© iStockphoto.com/Killerblo, 61
© iStockphoto.com/Nuno Silva, 81
© iStockphoto.com/oariff, 66
© iStockphoto.com/Oleg Prikhodko, 64
© iStockphoto.com/Petro Feketa, 28
© iStockphoto.com/Serdar Yagci, 23
© iStockphoto.com/track5, 47
© iStockphoto.com/Tracy Whiteside Photography, 69
© iStockphoto.com/webphotographeer, 78
Image copyright JJJ, 2008. Used under license from
    Shutterstock.com, 24
Image copyright Judex, 2008. Used under license from
    Shutterstock.com, 16
Image copyright Andrew Lever, 2008. Used under license
    from Shutterstock.com, 37
Image copyright Xavier Marchant, 2008. Used under license
    from Shutterstock.com, 31

About the Author

Jenny MacKay is an editor of books and journal articles and the author of several nonfiction books for teens, including *Fingerprinting*, *Criminal Profiling*, and *Amnesia*. She is currently pursuing her master's degree in creative writing. She lives with her husband and two children in northern Nevada, where she was born and raised.